TRADEMARKING YOUR BUSINESS

SUZANNE HARRINGTON

DISCLAIMER

Although the author and publisher have made every reasonable effort to ensure that the information in this book was correct at press time, neither the author nor the publisher can guarantee that everything in it is without flaw. They do not assume and hereby expressly disclaim any and all liability whatsoever to any party for any loss, damage, alleged libel or disruption caused by the contents or by error or omission of any kind whatsoever, whether such error or omission results from negligence, accident, or from any other cause.

Names and identifying details have been changed to protect the privacy of individuals.

The references to particular trade marks in this book are for the purpose of critique and review.

TESTIMONIALS

"Suzanne Harrington has written this no-nonsense, easy-to-follow guide to the complex and often misunderstood issue of trademarking. Condensing her decades of corporate experience, Suzanne lays out the facts and blows up the myths so you can avoid business name or product name identity theft, which means you'll save a lot of time and money.

"This handy book, Trademarking Your Business, *is recommended reading for all business owners to avoid the pitfalls of not trademarking your brands."*

Kathleen Ann
Owner/Marketing Strategist and Coach to Solopreneurs
Power Up Your Marketing
www.powerupyourmarketing.com.au

"As someone who has been helping people to set up and run their businesses for many years, it is always encouraging to see others also willing to help these businesses do it the right way. Suzanne is one of those people. While reading Suzanne's book, you'll learn disasters can happen if you don't take the time (and yes, money) to make sure your business name or product name is protected!

"We have all our business names (and some of our product names too!) trademarked and I recommend my clients do the same. Whether you are a solopreneur starting out or a more established SME, there is no

difference in the need to protect one of your most important business assets - your IP. If you want to learn how and why you can protect your brands and avoid being in the centre of a brand dispute, give Suzanne's book a read!"

Lara Kilborn
Business Development Manager
Business Enterprise Centre Southern Sydney Ltd
www.becsouthernsydney.com.au

"If you are a business person thinking that your brand is protected, but don't have trademark registration, then think again. That's where I was with my business, Personal Blooms, until I met Suzanne.

"She has inspired me and lots of my business colleagues to take that step to make sure you own and can protect your business from your competitors who might try to copy your brand. This is so important as your business grows and it is a step that many businesses fail to take.

"Anyone reading Suzanne's book, Trademarking Your Business, will be inspired, as I was, to ensure that their business brand is registered the right way, at the start of your business, and so have peace of mind that I now have."

Bibiana Beaupark
Owner, Personal Blooms
www.personalblooms.com.au

"I am passionate about helping managers and business owners to master people management skills, in particular, by empowering them to think and act successfully. Part of being successful is making the right decisions at the right time and this includes the decision to protect a valuable brand. Anyone in business and anyone who values their brand or product needs to think of protection.

"I would recommend Suzanne for expert assistance in trademarking your brand or brands and taking action to avoid being in any of the disaster stories outlined in her book, Trademarking Your Business."

Sally Foley Lewis
Management Trainer and Workplace Coach
Creator of Management Success Cards
Author of *Successful Feedback*
www.managementsuccesscards.com.au

"In our business, Success Women's Network, I work with women who want more out of life than just being employed – women who want a hand to grow a successful business. This is an exciting time for them, but there is a lot for them to learn.

"Suzanne has been part of our group for nearly 2 years and has helped so many of our members get ownership of their business names through trademarking. She has educated them on the benefits of owning and protecting their business names and product names, so they can avoid the horror stories that can happen if you don't trademark your name and some of these stories are outlined in her book, Trademarking Your Business. This is a must read if you want to get your business off on the

right foot, and also for those who already run a successful business, but who have not yet taken this important step."

Natalie Moutia
Owner, Success Women's Network
Business Coach
www.successwomensnetwork.com.au

"I first met Suzanne through one of our local networking groups and immediately thought that trademarking our brand, BOLD TRAIL-ERS, was something we needed to do. The need to protect our brand became more evident when we noticed people taking photos of our branding, products and logo at trade expos. It was refreshing to find that Suzanne would take care of all the hassle and gently guide us through the trademarking process, without the headache that I thought it was going to be.

"We now have our brand safe and secure and we would highly recommend other businesses do the same thing, i.e. trademark their brands sooner, rather than later. Suzanne's book answers a lot of the questions that we had and many readers will have too. To avoid being involved in a horror story of your own with your brands - read the book, Trademarking Your Business, and get your brands registered as trademarks."

Jaclyn Bold
Co-Founder of Bold Trailers
www.boldtrailers.com.au
CEO of Bold Connections
www.boldconnections.com

"From the viewpoint of someone who has protected her brand through Suzanne's services and who coaches people to be the best they can, I would highly recommend learning how to avoid having a business name or product name stolen by a competitor by reading Suzanne's book, Trademarking Your Business, and learning from other's mistakes! You will find that the questions you have been asking yourself about trademarks are answered for you."

Julie White
Develop Beyond
Author of *Develop Beyond*
www.developbeyond.com.au

"We at MPM FINANCIAL GROUP first saw Suzanne's comments on brand protection on a social media site and without hesitation we thought 'we need to protect our brand and need Pinnacle TMS to do it'. We have worked so hard for our brand and with all the social media available we certainly didn't want anyone stealing our ideas. So, we engaged Suzanne from Pinnacle TMS to help us. We found working with Suzanne was a breath of fresh air. She made everything simple for us and was professional at all times. We can't recommend her highly enough!

"In our business of working with people to improve their financial wellbeing, we know the value of good advice and in Suzanne's approach you will not be disappointed. Businesses of all sizes can benefit from knowing the answers to the trademark questions

outlined in Suzanne's book, Trademarking Your Business, to make sure they are ticking off the boxes to own and protect their brands."

Paula Mezrani
Founder MPM Financial Group
www.mpmfg.com.au

I dedicate this book to my wonderful husband, Martin, and to my family who have supported and encouraged me with my new change in career.

I am so grateful to be surrounded by such a loving family and many caring friends, both personal and professional; some of whom have pushed me forward when I was very happy to stand back.

Thank you all so much!

"If you build it, they will come"

- adapted from the book *Field of Dreams* by W. P. Kinsella

FORWARD

I have purposely written this book to be an informal read for business people.

It is not meant to be legal advice in any way, shape or form; and nor is it a comprehensive book on all issues related to trademarks.

I have tried to keep this book as an easy tool to alert business owners and their advisors to the traps they can fall into by not thinking of registering their brand or brands as trademarks. I have provided answers, as basically as possible, for the most often asked questions relating to trademarks.

Providing some disaster stories and tips on how to avoid them just helps bring home that disasters can and does happen to many businesses, but there are steps that can and should be taken to avoid them.

Each person reading this book will need to seek specific trademark advice to suit his or her particular needs. It's important to make sure the person giving the advice has the specialised knowledge needed to deal with trademarks and that it's something they do every day; not just a few times a year!

I hope that the information contained in this book gets people thinking more of the importance of trademarking their brands, and that brands are a valuable business asset to own and protect.

Happy reading!

CONTENTS

INTRODUCTION

Many people start a business without considering trademark protection and this can be incredibly dangerous. In fact, certain breaches of the Australian Trade Marks Act 1995 constitute criminal offences with penalties of sentences up to two years and fines of up to $55,000.

So why is it that so many business owners overlook this area when they start their business?

I am passionate about helping business owners avoid penalties and secure the future for themselves and their business. So I am writing this book to share with you how you can get your business off on the right foot – from Day 1.

Whether you are a solopreneur, a small to medium sized business or a large business with many brands, it is important to consider brand protection at all levels.

My name is Suzanne Harrington and I am the Director and Trademark Manager of Pinnacle TMS.

By way of background: I have worked for Australian top tier law firms for over 20 years in brand registration and trademark portfolio management, both in Australia and internationally. I have worked with a vast range of clients from multinational Australian household brands with billions of dollars' turnover, right through to IT startup companies where the company was operating from a garage.

Some of those clients you will have heard of, such as Qantas®, Primo Smallgoods®, Optus® and American Express®. Working with these larger clients was mostly through either in-house lawyers or external lawyers who were familiar with the trademark process and the importance of brand protection.

There was never a question of whether a brand would be trademarked and protected – it was just: 'If the brand is available, protect it!'

But what about these?

These are small businesses whose owners have understood the importance of protecting their business name or product name from the word go.

I have worked with all of these businesses and brand protection is just as important for smaller businesses starting out as it is for the mega corporations.

As you can imagine, while focusing on trademarks over the years, I have gained experience in all aspects of trademark registration and renewal, as well as other related services such as recording assignments, following acquisitions and recording changes to an owner's name and/or address.

Why the change? After so long in the corporate law firm environment, I was enjoying what I did, but not so much the environment - as I'm sure some of you will appreciate. So I started looking for a change and saw a gap in the marketplace for providing trademark services to small and medium-sized businesses. Also, in the current economic climate, there are larger companies wishing to find a more cost-effective way of managing their trademark portfolios and a boutique company like mine fits that bill.

So I took the plunge and started Pinnacle TMS to fill that gap and work with people and SMEs to get their brands protected – even when they don't know they need it!

Let's move on now to looking at what business owners want and need to know to protect one of their most important assets – their brand or brands.

By understanding more about the importance and process of trademarks, business owners will be able to make those informed decisions which could mean the difference between owning their brands and losing their businesses!

Are you the person who advises your clients regarding starting up a business? Or perhaps are a graphic artist who creates brands for your clients. Your clients will be impressed if you can offer valuable insight that could one day save their business.

Educating business owners on the importance of trademarks for their business can be very satisfying. When people save thousands of dollars by avoiding infringing someone else's trademark, or they can quickly take steps to stop a competitor using their brand by relying on their trademark registration, that makes it all the more satisfying!

I received a referral from a lawyer in a legal firm a few weeks ago, who I had spoken to about 12 months ago. At that time he seemed to be very interested in the services I offered and how my services would complement the services offered to their clients. However, I didn't hear anything from him until a few weeks ago – when he referred a business client to me.

I have to say that I thought this was quite interesting. It seemed strange that the law firm had either not had any business clients for 12 months (which would have been very difficult for them to still be in business) or that the lawyer must have thought this particular business client was really special to come to me.

In fact, trademark registration and protection is a vital step for all businesses, particularly when they are starting out or releasing a new product.

Can you put a value on your business brand or your business product? How much time, money and effort will you put into your brand and trying to establish a reputation in your industry?

In this book I am going to share with you:

- the top 10 questions I am asked about trademark protection

- information and tips that you will be able to use

- triggers for you to start thinking: 'I need to protect this!'

I am also going to share some disaster stories with you, so you can learn how to avoid them.

Hopefully when you have read this book you will realise that trademarking a business name or product name is one of the first (and most important) steps a business owner can and should take.

If you are a business advisor, you will also be able to pass this knowledge on to your clients and network, to help them avoid being in the centre of these disaster stories themselves!

CHAPTER 1

WHAT IS A TRADEMARK?

A trademark can be a word or words, phrases, symbols, designs, or a combination of these elements, to identify and distinguish the goods or services of one party from those of another.

In everyday life you will know and use many examples of each of these types of brands:

QANTAS ®   **BILLABONG**®   **GOOGLE**®

The owners of these brands know the value of trademark registration so that competitors can't copy their branding without the owner being able to sue for infringement. They also understand that these brands are **valuable assets** to their businesses.

Trademarks can also be smells, sounds, non-English words, numbers and even musical jingles.

You have probably noticed how people are attracted to famous brands, and how those brands can cut across borders, cultures and languages, so that what might originate in one part of the world can be used and recognised on the other side of the world.

Some of those brands are Apple, McDonald's and Revlon. When someone talks about any of these brands, you instantly know whether they represent products or services you are willing to pay a certain price for.

Trademarks can be used on products and services, and often on a combination of those.

As far as the public is concerned, trademarks help prevent confusion in the marketplace, so that a purchaser can make a decision to purchase a product or service based on what they know of the brand or what they have heard or read about the brand.

From a business owner's perspective, this is of huge value - because often a purchaser is willing to pay a premium to purchase the 'must have' brand.

TIP: Check with a trademark specialist on whether your brand can be registered as a trademark – don't assume anything.

CHAPTER 2

IS A TRADEMARK THE SAME AS A BUSINESS NAME?

While a business name is often used as a brand or trademark, having business name registration does not give you ownership of that name. It is simply a government requirement so that people can find out who is behind a particular name, but does not give you brand ownership.

Imagine if you started using a new business name and six months later (or even years later), you received a letter from a competitor or a lawyer to say you had to change your name or be sued.

How would you feel about that? What would it cost you to rebrand?

My client, Janet*, learnt this the hard way ... this is her story.

Janet had been using her brand, which was also her business name, for nearly 8 years.

She had worked hard to build her reputation and believed that her business name and brand were hers - particularly as she had been using it for so long. Business was looking good — more clients were referring business to her and she was becoming well known in her industry.

With her business growing, Janet was on top of the world!

Out of the blue, Janet received a letter from a lawyer instructing her to stop using the name, because his client had a trademark registration for that brand and Janet was infringing that client's trademark rights.

At first Janet didn't believe that this was right – she owned the business name, didn't she? It was registered with the relevant government authority and had been for some time, so what was this all about?!

For Janet, receiving a letter like this was emotionally draining and took the focus off her main game of building her business.

The letter said that Janet basically had to stop using the brand as her business name, on her website, and on her marketing material – everywhere - otherwise she would be sued and lose the business that she built with her own blood, sweat and tears!

Janet told me that she had not taken this lying down. She had been fighting against the change for 6 months because she believed she had been doing the right thing and had many clients who knew her and her business.

6 months later, feeling drained and frustrated with the fight, she had finally decided she had had wasted enough time, money and energy (not to mention sleep!) and decided to rebrand and stop using her current name as the lawyers had requested.

*Janet learnt the hard way that she could have avoided all this pain and heartache, if she organised for the right research to be done **before** starting her business. Having her brand trademarked at that stage would have meant that she owned it!*

When Janet called me, although she was still emotionally attached to her old name, she had decided on a new name and wanted me to do the research to make sure the name was available for her to use, and then start the trademarking process as soon as possible.

One thing Janet knew for sure was that she didn't want to end up in the same position again!

The good news for Janet is that her new name was unique enough to go smoothly through the registration process. Now she has peace of mind that she owns the brand and won't end up in the same position down the track.

So the question of whether a trademark is the same as a business name is an important one for business owners, and one that is often answered incorrectly.

It is possible, with many years of use, to gain what is called 'common law rights' in a name/brand if you have not taken steps to register it as a trademark.

The problem with that is that proving those rights to stop a competitor from copying your brand can be incredibly expensive! It takes time and money to put together evidence of years of use and then provide that evidence in legal documents, etc.

Why would you rely on this process when it is so inexpensive to simply register the brand and own it?

If you register your brand, you won't be sued for trademark infringement and risk losing your business – also, you can avoid business name or product name identity theft.

Having a trademark registration gives you exclusive rights to use the name, so you can stop your competitors from copying you and trading on your reputation.

This really should be a no-brainer for a business owner that is spending thousands of dollars in setup costs and marketing!

> TIP: As soon as you choose a name and **before** you do any marketing, web design, etc., get an Initial Protection Review and Strategy Report done so you know whether you can actually use and register the name as a trademark.

CHAPTER 3

WHAT IS THE DIFFERENCE BETWEEN ™ AND ® SYMBOLS? DO I HAVE TO USE EITHER?

Business owners often get confused between these symbols, but there is a BIG difference between them:

'TM' stands for Trade Mark. This symbol can indicate that you have a pending application for the brand, or you are claiming some rights in the name without trademark registration.

Businesses use this symbol to indicate protection of a brand, but that protection is not ownership and is often misleading.

It can be a useful tool to show your competitors you have at least thought of trademark protection, but if it came down to a challenge, you would not have the full rights of a registered trademark.

'R' stands for registered. The ® symbol, on the other hand, indicates the trademark is registered and the owner has exclusive rights to the mark.

Using this symbol means you are serious about your brand and can take action against a competitor who likes your great brand and thinks it would be good for his or her business too!

It is also important to know the difference, and that the use of this symbol without actually having the brand registered as a trademark is misleading and deceptive; if challenged, severe penalties can be imposed.

I would highly recommend that you don't take the risk of being caught using this symbol if you don't actually have a trademark registration for the particular brand.

There is no legal requirement to use either symbol. But if you are serious about your brand and value it, it is a natural progression to have it registered and then use the ® symbol.

Using that symbol lets your competitors know you value the brand and could take action against them, including suing for trademark infringement.

TIPS:
- If your trademark is registered in the relevant country, use the ® symbol on all your advertising.
- If your trademark is not registered in the relevant country, use the ™ symbol.

CHAPTER 4

CAN I JUST SEARCH MYSELF TO SEE IF SOMEONE ELSE HAS A TRADEMARK REGISTRATION FOR MY PROPOSED BRAND?

The simple answer is 'yes'. There is a government register you can search. In Australia it's called ATMOSS. Most other countries have their own Registers that can be researched.

But this is John's story when he did the research himself …

John*, a businessman I met recently, told me he chose a business name for his new business, and did the checks he thought he needed to do. He then did as all business owners do: spent time and money on his website, marketing, accountants and lawyers to set up his business framework, etc.

John was confident he had done all he needed to do to own his brand, so he went about building his business and his reputation.

Within six months, John had lost it all. Why? He received a letter from a lawyer acting for a barrister who had a registered trademark for a similar name in the same industry.

The letter threatened him with action, including suing him personally, for any loss the barrister might incur as a result of John using a brand that was similar to the barrister's trademark.

Imagine John's horror! He thought he'd done the right searches to confirm no one else had the same name, but didn't realise that having a business name registration didn't give him ownership of the name.

*What was also strange to John was that although they were in the same industry, the barrister's trademark was not the same as his brand. What John didn't know was if a business has a **similar** trademark registered in the same industry, that is all that is needed to stop a likely competitor from using the brand. If they refuse, then as the owner of the trademark, you have the option to sue.*

John decided not to fight the demand and basically handed the name over.

John told me he was emotionally devastated to receive that letter and had no idea that this could happen! He was also grateful that he'd not spent more time growing the business and ploughing more money into marketing because he would have lost much more.

*John learnt a valuable lesson and with any new venture, he will include having the name checked by a trademark specialist who knows what to look for **before** he starts spending money on it.*

So while you can do your own research, there is a 'but'. Do you understand what you are looking for? Trademark infringement includes use of marks that are *similar*. You need to see, assess and base the safety of your business on the decision you make on that information.

You may have a name; say for instance, Unicorn Clothing Shop. You look at the Trademarks Register and find another brand: Unicorn Shoes & Accessories. Different brands, right?

The answer is 'No' – because under Trademark Law, both of these marks would be taken to be 'Unicorn'. The other words are just descriptors. Both marks would cover products in at least the same class, and often shops sell clothing, shoes and accessories under the one brand.

So using a trademark searching specialist will help you avoid making a costly error in knowing the difference.

When filing a trademark application, you also need to know which of the 45 classes of goods/services are relevant to you and your business now and into the near future.

Classes are 'associated' with each other – do you know which ones are relevant to what your business does?

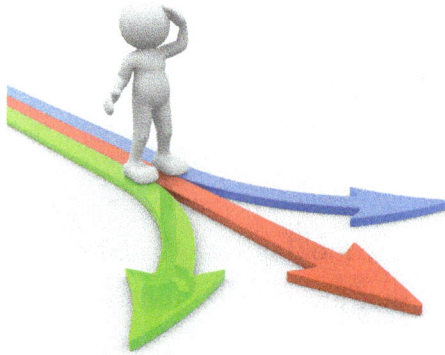

TIPS:
- Although you can do a knockout initial search, don't rely on your search to build your brand.
- Using the services of a trademark specialist will provide you with peace of mind that your brand is safe to use and register.

CHAPTER 5

WHY WOULD I USE A SPECIALIST TO REGISTER A TRADEMARK, RATHER THAN DO IT MYSELF?

A trademark specialist knows what to do and will provide options and strategies for responding to the examiner. This will hopefully get the application through and achieve the best result for your brand. Often there are a number of issues to be addressed and it can seem like a maze, but that is where a trademark specialist will help with their knowledge of the system.

This is Rosemary's* story on filing her trademark application …

Rosemary came to me with an application she had filed herself which covered 2 service classes for business coaching. The Trademarks Office examiner had rejected the application and she wanted to know if I could help her overcome that rejection.

I was able to give Rosemary some strategies and options to consider, but I saw she had not covered two other classes for products that she was likely to have in her business; e.g. computer software and printed matter she also branded and sold.

Because you can't add further classes to an application once it is filed, a fresh application had to be filed to protect those products. This involved further costs, which could have been avoided had Rosemary known and understood the trademark classification system.

So it's similar to doing your own tax return, or will, or website – can you achieve the best result for your business?

This is Paul's* story on an application he had filed …

Paul is a small business owner who had filed an application for his brand. He thought it was all finished and he didn't need my help.

When I looked at the details of his application on the Trademarks Office Register, Paul had not paid the registration fee and had only two weeks left to pay it or his application would lapse and not be registered at all!

Paul thought all he had to pay was the filing fee and he did not bother reading the information about paying the registration fee within the relevant timeframe. Had I not checked, Paul wouldn't have known and his brand would not have been protected.

How would Paul have felt if he needed to stop a competitor from copying his brand?!

Another circumstance is when a person files a trademark application and the Trademarks Office examiner rejects the application.

Often, business owners don't know what to do and simply put it in the 'too-hard' basket. This results in their application lapsing so there is no trademark registration and the business brand is vulnerable to being copied by a competitor.

The other issue that crops up regularly is business owners trying to cut costs by filing their own trademark applications, particularly when a business is starting up; i.e. cutting costs on protecting their brand because it can look deceptively easy to do.

The good thing is that they will have some protection if they do get their trademark through the registration process.

But because a trademark specialist works with the system every day, they can provide you with options and strategies (that you may otherwise be unaware of) to achieve the best result for your business.

For instance, there are standard applications, head start applications, expedited examinations of applications – which option is best for you and your business? And what are the differences? Why would you use one option over another

Consider that your brand is what you will be working hard to build a reputation in, so that your customers or clients will know you and what your brand stands for. Why would you take the risk of not doing it right in the first place, especially when the cost is probably less than what you will pay for some of your office furniture?!

There are other risks too …

For instance, you could under-protect your brand by not covering the right classes, or your application could lapse because you are not aware of the timeframes within the trademark application process. Neither is a good result for your brand.

After all, the money you invest now will protect your brand for at least 10 years, and for each 10 period thereafter, as long as you continue to pay the renewal fees.

A warning though: the 'use it or lose it' rule can apply here if your trademark is challenged.

TIP:
- Filing a trademark application is not as simple as you might think and you risk not covering your brand in the right classes.
- If your mark is unique in your industry, get registration of the word/s, rather than a combination of word/s and a logo, for the broadest protection.
- Because your brand will need to cover what you are doing now and also what your business will do in the near future, really think about what you want the business to be doing so the right classes are included in your registration.

CHAPTER 6

IF I CHOOSE A NAME, MAY I JUST USE IT WITHOUT TRADEMARK REGISTRATION? WHAT HAPPENS IF I DON'T REGISTER MY BRAND AS A TRADEMARK?

These questions again have a 'Yes' answer - but with a caveat. If you do this, you run the risk of using a brand that someone else has already registered, so you could be sued for trademark infringement and even lose your business.

Or you could establish the business through years of hard work, only to see one of your competitors copy your brand. It would then be up to you to prove that you had sufficient reputation in the brand to stop the competitor from using the same (or something very similar) because it was causing confusion in the marketplace.

This is Alison's story ...

Alison* came to me because she had received a letter from someone telling her that she was infringing his trademark registration. He offered to license the use of his mark to her, but otherwise she had to stop using the name she had been using for 18 months.

As you can imagine, Alison was not happy about this!

*Alison had only done business name searches and found that no one had the **same** name as the one she had chosen.*

She saw that there were a few names that were similar, so she added a word and it was registered as a business name – great! – Alison had her name and off she went building her business.

So when Alison received this letter she was at first surprised, then thought: 'No way! This is my name and I'm using it.'

Alison didn't understand that had she had some trademark specialist research done on the name, she would have been told that someone else had a trademark registration for a very similar name in the same industry. That would have automatically sent warning bells about that name and she would have avoided the stress and costs of the position in which she now found herself.

Having been alerted to the fact that there was already a trademark registration for that brand for the same services, Alison could have chosen another name for her business.

After discussing the options and the costs to fight, Alison decided to rebrand.

There is a happy ending to this story! During the rebranding process, Alison decided to expand her target market; which she would not have been able to do with the brand she had been using.

The whole experience was not good for her budget; nor was the distraction from her business a good thing.

Having to change your brand can be a very expensive and time-consuming exercise that can easily be avoided by setting up your business brand in the right way from Day 1.

The same rule applies not only for your business name but also for book titles, computer apps, food products, and clothing brands – basically any product that has a great unique name!

TIPS:
- Ensure you are not naming a business or product with a trademark that is already owned by someone else in your industry.
- Ensure you file the right trademark application to make sure you own the name and can protect it from your competitors.

CHAPTER 7

DOESN'T IT COST THOUSANDS OF DOLLARS TO REGISTER?

Currently, on average, from filing to registration for one class, you would allow around AU$1400 for a 10 year registration, with no further fees to pay during that timeframe.

Is that too much for peace of mind?

Kim* called me saying she was interested in using my services because she had a great brand and wanted to own and be able to protect it.

I outlined the costs involved, but Kim thought in the end she could save money by doing it herself.

When I looked at the application Kim had filed, she had only covered the clothes, not the retailing or wholesaling of the clothes - so she had not fully protected her brand.

As well, Kim did have a unique name as she said, which she could have protected alone. But Kim didn't understand the trademark system, so she filed the application covering a combination of the name and a logo, which narrowed the protection the eventual registration gave her.

The cost will depend on the type of business you have and how the trademark will be used. If you have a business with lots of branded products as well as services you provide, then more classes will need to be covered and the more expensive it will be, because the cost increases per class.

But the question and bottom line should really be: 'What will it cost me if I **don't** own my brand? Can I afford to stop a competitor from stealing my brand and customers?'!

> TIPS:
> - Trademark registration is not expensive, especially compared to ongoing business expenses.
> - Trademarking your business name adds value to your business – it's a business asset.

CHAPTER 8

ONCE I REGISTER MY TRADEMARK IN AUSTRALIA, IS IT COVERED OVERSEAS?

The short answer to this question is 'No' - a trademark registration only covers the country in which you applied.

Jason* is looking to export his products and go into the US market and later into Europe. He wants to know how he can protect his brand with those plans in mind.

Using a system called the Madrid Protocol and the Australian application or registration as a base, it is possible to file an application in other countries as and when the business grows. This will allow Jason to take a step-by-step approach to protecting his brand around the world.

This can be particularly important for businesses when budgeting for overseas expansion of their brand or brands.

It also helps in being more efficient and cost-effective when renewing and making any changes to the registration.

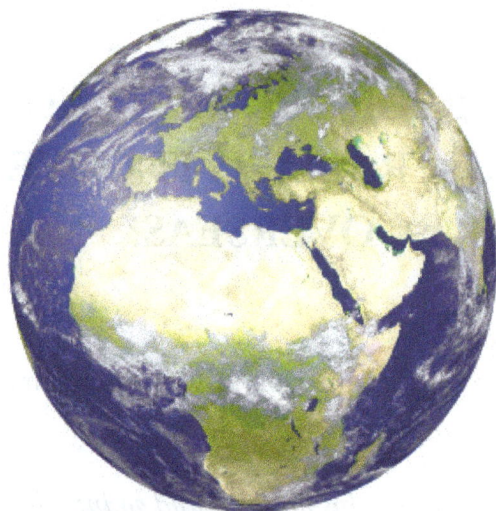

The Madrid Protocol process enables you to nominate the countries you want to cover in one application. The application will still be examined by the individual country's Trademark Office to make sure it qualifies under their law and that no prior registrations exists.

It is also possible to cover all 28 countries that (currently) make up the European Community.

TIP:
- Trademark registration is generally done on a country-by-country basis.
- There are other ways of filing one or two applications to cover a number of countries around the world.

CHAPTER 9

WHAT DO I NEED TO DO IF I AM EXPORTING INTO ANOTHER COUNTRY?

Peter*, the owner of a medium sized business, decided to protect one of their premier brands in New Zealand as they were doing a lot of business in that market.

What research showed, however, was that a distributor of their product had registered the brand as a trademark in New Zealand without Peter's knowledge.

This came as a shock, as it had not occurred to Peter that a distributor would claim ownership of the brand. So Peter had to hire a lawyer to enter into negotiations to get his company's own brand back!

The lesson here is to ensure your trademark is registered in the market in which your products are being sold. And, if you have a distributor, to make sure they are aware of your ownership and use the brand according to your instructions.

This is another step that business owners often fail to take when looking at a new market.

If you start using your brand in another country, without researching whether a competitor has already registered the same (or a similar) brand in that country, you run the risk of being sued for trademark infringement in that country.

If research shows that the mark is available to use and register, it should also be trademarked there. For instance, if you decide to enter the New Zealand market, and you go ahead without doing searches, you could find you receive a letter from a lawyer to say you are infringing their client's brand in that country, even though it may be registered as a trademark in Australia.

While trademarking your business name in each country you want to enter can be expensive and time consuming, it can be disastrous if you find yourself in a brand dispute in a foreign country.

Working out a budget for entering other countries should be part of your brand protection strategy.

TIPS:
- Make sure the right research is done to ensure you are not using a trademark that is already owned by someone else in your industry in the country you are entering. You may have to change the brand in other jurisdictions.
- Trademark the brand to make sure you own and can protect it in the country you are entering.

CHAPTER 10

OKAY – I KNOW I SHOULD TRADEMARK MY BRAND, SO CAN YOU DO IT STRAIGHTAWAY THIS WEEK?

Unfortunately, the trademark registration process generally takes a minimum of 7-8 months from the date of filing. In some countries the timeframe can be much longer. Timing varies from country to country, but you can expect that it is certainly not a quick process.

Cathy* came to me initially to protect the name of one of her businesses. She had selected a name for another business, but decided to hold off for the time being and just register the one name. Cathy had done her *own search and found nothing like it on the Register so was happy to hold off.*

A few months later, Cathy called me and said she was ready to go ahead, but she had just done another search and someone had filed an application in the last few weeks that was nearly the same as hers, for the same type of business!

I did some research and found that yes, it was going to be an issue and that Cathy would need to choose another name or be prepared to spend lots of money on trying to overcome objections from the Trademarks Office. She could also have run the risk of getting in a dispute with the owner of the other similar brand.

Cathy said she would go back to the drawing board and come up with another name. Lesson learnt! Once you have a name you really like, have it researched and then file for it. Don't wait!

The timing from filing to registration can also depend on whether the relevant Trademarks Office raises any issues when the application is examined to make sure it complies with relevant rules.

The good news is that in most countries, once you gain registration and ownership of your brand, it is backdated to the date the application was filed.

Although the trademark registration process is lengthy, there are ways to minimise the time to know whether you are at least likely to gain registration of your brand.

Also, just because the trademarking process is lengthy, does not mean you should not do it. Trademarking your business name is an important step regardless of how long it takes.

The lesson is: file as soon as you can, because if you don't, someone else might - and then your application would not get through and you may need to start from scratch and find another brand!

TIPS:
- Trademark registration is a lengthy process.
- There are processes to find out where you stand with a brand in a relatively short time, although the final registration may take some time.
- The **filing date** is the important date. Once research shows the brand is cleared, have a trademark application filed straightaway before a competitor can file a brand that might block your brand from going through to registration.

A QUICK CHECKLIST COMPARING

REGISTRATION AND NON-REGISTRATION

TRADEMARKS USED WITHOUT REGISTRATION	REGISTERED TRADEMARKS
No proprietary rights in the name	Full proprietary rights including the right to sue, licence or sell the trademark
Business name/company registration required to be renewed at regular periods, paying additional fees each time	Trademark registration period is for 10 years with no further fees payable until the end of that period, then a renewal fee needs to be paid
Has value only as part of the business/company as a whole	Trademark can have its own value which can be sold or licensed/ franchised separately
Business name registration now Australia-wide but similar names can coexist in the marketplace	Trademark registration is Australia-wide – exclusive rights to the same or similar name in your industry
If action is taken against someone using the same (or a similar) trademark, evidence is required to support such action and is time-consuming and expensive	Action can readily be taken for infringement of a registered trademark that is the same or similar in your industry

ABOUT THE AUTHOR

Suzanne Harrington is a Trademark Specialist and one of Australia's leading Trademark Registration Strategists. Her years of experience in dealing with the registration process, both in Australia and around the world, have enabled Suzanne to develop an enviable reputation for dealing effectively and efficiently with the Australian Trade Marks Office. The result is that Suzanne can achieve registration of her clients' trademarks and so be responsive to her clients' needs.

Suzanne has a wealth of knowledge in dealing successfully with overseas trademark attorneys and IP specialists to secure brand protection in countries around the globe.

Suzanne started her own company in 2010 after seeing a niche in the marketplace where small to medium sized businesses were not being provided with knowledge about protecting their names; leaving them vulnerable to business name or product name identity theft.

Suzanne's mission is to provide options and strategies to businesses so that they have the knowledge to own and protect their most valuable assets: their brands. Through her company, Pinnacle TMS Pty Ltd, she is able to do just that!

Personally, Suzanne is married to Martin and is the mother of three boys and three stepdaughters. During her spare time, Suzanne enjoys dancing and painting to release the artistic side of her nature. Travelling is also one of the big highlights of Suzanne's life and she takes the opportunity to travel whenever she can.

You can email Suzanne at info@pinnacletms.com.au or visit the website at www.pinnacletms.com.au

FOOTNOTE:

The trademarks listed in this book are the registered trademarks of:

Apple Inc.

BP p.l.c.

Weber-Stephen Products LLC

Nike International Ltd

Southcorp Brands Pty Ltd

GSM (Trademarks) Pty Ltd

Qantas Airways Ltd

Google Inc

Bibiana Beaupark

ASCII Computer Training Centre Pty Ltd

www.ingramcontent.com/pod-product-compliance
Lightning Source LLC
Chambersburg PA
CBHW070410200326
41518CB00011B/2149